MA Ingle.

D0307175

LETTERCRAFT

Tony Hart

LETTERCRAFT

Guild Publishing London

To Will, Carolyn and 'Hattie'

This edition published 1986 by
Book Club Associates
by arrangement with
William Heinemann Ltd

First published 1986
Copyright © Tony Hart 1986

Photoset by Rowland Phototypesetting Ltd,
Bury St Edmunds, Suffolk
Printed in Great Britain by
Springbourne Press Ltd

Contents

Introduction

For centuries the simple shapes of squares, triangles and circles have been used repetitiously to create geometric patterns. The beautiful Cufic writing of Islam has for thousands of years been used to decorate traditional objects as well as the Mosques. The Mixtec writing of South America and the Hieroglyphs of Ancient Egypt were seen as pictures and the brush characters of the Orient are still works of art.

For this book I have designed a European alphabet, based on the Roman letter, which can be used to make patterns, designs and graphic illustrations to please the eye in a similar way. All the letters can be treated as units that fit together and assume an integral shape. The combinations and permutations of the letter forms are never-ending and the colourful patterns and designs you can create can be applied in many craft areas, for example, to decorate pottery, stationery, needle-work, knitting, wood and metalwork.

This unorthodox craft of lettering can be enjoyed by anyone of any age, from the very young who are still learning to identify and write the letters of the alphabet to those who wish to find ways of adding interest and originality to whatever craft they follow. Those who decide to try pattern making just for fun will, I believe, be pleasantly surprised at their own creative abilities.

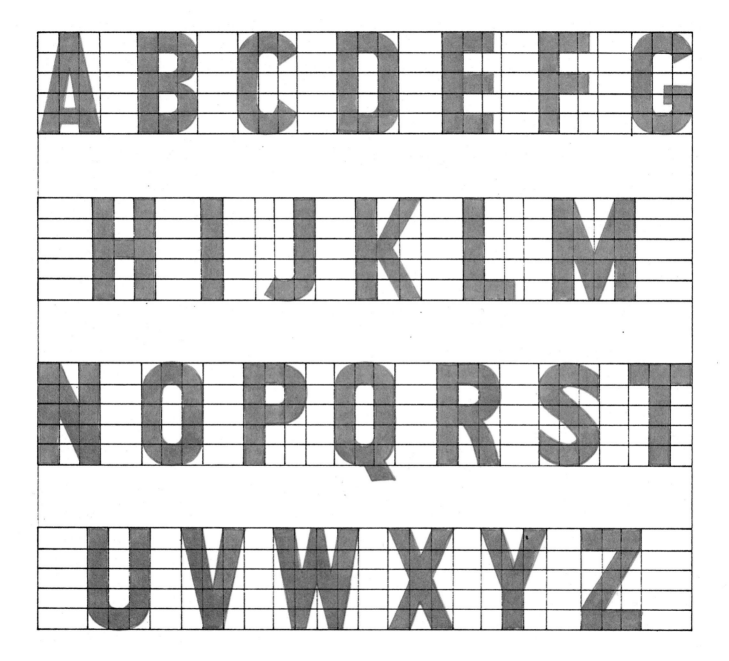

The letters of the alphabet shown here were designed specially for Lettercraft pattern making and drawn within a number of small squares. All the letters are five squares high. The I is one square wide. Most letters are three wide but E, F, L and J are two and a half wide. M and W are shown as four wide. W can be five by five, making it in a square. It's a matter of choice.

In general the bowls of curved letters like B, R, P and O are not really half circles but have been slightly flattened. The O shown here is more rectangular with curved corners.

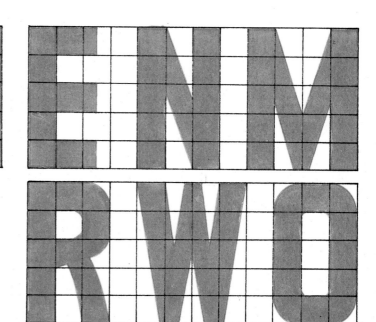

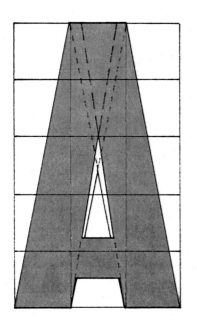

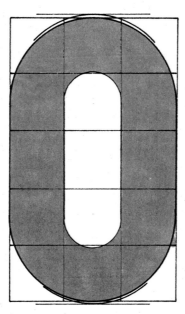

Letters with V shaped angles, A, W, Y, K, if drawn with parallel lines will look heavy at the apex. If the lines are drawn to meet further away the letter will look better. You can see how this has been done in drawing the large A.

Should you wish to draw O's with half circles at top and base you should extend the bowls very slightly over the base and top lines, otherwise an optical illusion makes the letter look shorter. These adjustments are for perfectionists. When you draw your freehand letters you'll find yourself making these automatically. The only rule is: If it doesn't look right it isn't right.

A B C D E F G

H I J K L M

N O P Q R S T

U V W X Y Z

The alphabet on the opposite page has been drawn freehand. It looks freehand and it's meant to; neat, but drawn without ruler or compass.

First let's look at what the letters can do. These have something in common. They look the same upside down.

Some letters, those I've coloured orange on these pages, are symetrical; that is they mirror themselves if they are divided down the middle. There are eleven of these and they can be useful for all sorts of repetitive patterns. You will tend to use them most.

A few letters can be made to interlock and all letters can abut or make contact one way or another. It's easy to see the two E's but were they painted black it would be difficult to determine which letters were making that shape. The same applies to the other shapes.

The W and K make pleasant two unit patterns. The W's are put together sideways but there are several alternatives using just those two letters. The K on the far right is not necessarily a mirror image; it's an upside down K.

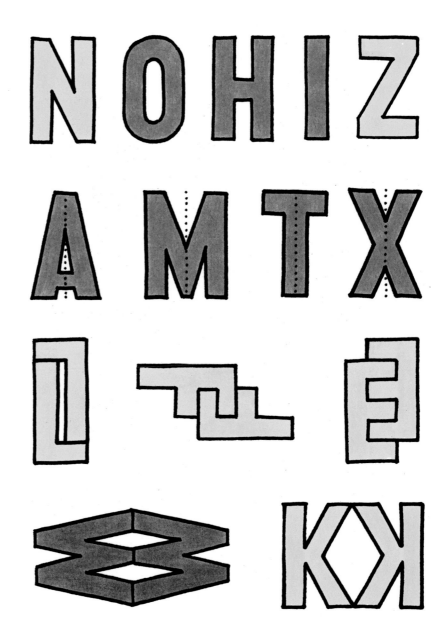

Reproducing the letter forms can be done in several ways. The most usual is to trace them from one of the alphabets provided in the book. At some stage you may wish to design your own. The method is to trace your letters, using a soft pencil, onto detail or some thin paper which it is possible to see through. This method enables you to reposition the tracing paper at different angles and draw the letters in the desired position. By using pencil, mistakes can be rectified before the pattern is gone over with pen or marker. A permanent marker is advised as the letters can be colourwashed without causing the letter lines to run. Should you wish to transfer the design to thicker paper or any other flat surface this should be done at the finished pencil stage, tracing through carbon paper or using coloured chalk dust on the back of the pencil drawing. Although rulers and compass pens can be useful I find that a freehand tracing and drawing has a far less mechanical effect, is more pleasing and far quicker. You will, however, find a protractor useful for finding those angles that form pentagons, hexagons, etc, but all the drawing in this book has been done freehand.

An alternative to tracing letters is to cut out stencils from thin card. If carefully cut, the letters can be used to draw round or the actual cutout letter for the stencil can be used. The disadvantage is that the stencil or cutout letter will not last very long. Also the stencil will have those middle bits missing as in O, D, B.

In the book you will find suggested patterns to make with one letter unit or more. You will soon want to make up your own designs but use the basic constructions from the book. As you become more interested and adept you will be experimenting with more complicated patterns. It's original and great fun to use your own initials in designing patterns that you can use for an unlimited series of personal items. Monograms are nothing new but to have a knitted garment with a pattern comprised of your initials is original. This also applies to rug making, designs in wood, marquetry, glassware and anything else.

The most entertaining characters can be created by using letter forms. There is a whole sequence devoted to freestyle letter forms where you can distort letters sufficiently to make them shape themselves as you want but never to become unreadable. This can provide an original form of illustration with creations not so geometric in appearance as those made with more formal letters.

Browsing through the book you will realise that it caters for those artists who prefer more freedom to express their ideas, while those who like precise draughtsmanship and geometric shapes will find much to satisfy them.

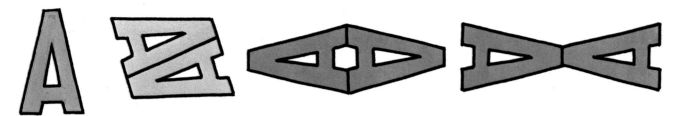

Here are some examples of letter patterns formed by connecting just two letters. There are more ways of joining the letter A's than shown here, but these are probably the most effective. The first example of sideways A's bring both top and bottom lines parallel. A repeat line of this pattern would make a useful frieze. The second shows how a third 'window' is made by connecting the A's base to base.

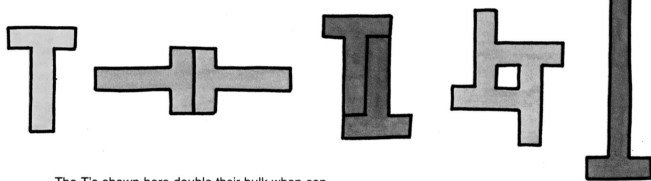

The T's shown here double their bulk when connected top to top or side to side. The other examples open out when connected by one third of the width. By leaving out the lines of connection the letters forming the design become less obvious and the design more interesting. Compare the final E pattern with that on page 11.

Shapes made up from three letter forms can be most effective based on an equilateral triangle. This can be formed by drawing a line through the centre of a circle and finding the angle of 120°. This goes three times into the circle. Where the lines from the centre meet the circumference are the points to be connected to make the triangle. Another interesting pattern is made by connecting three C's as shown at bottom left.

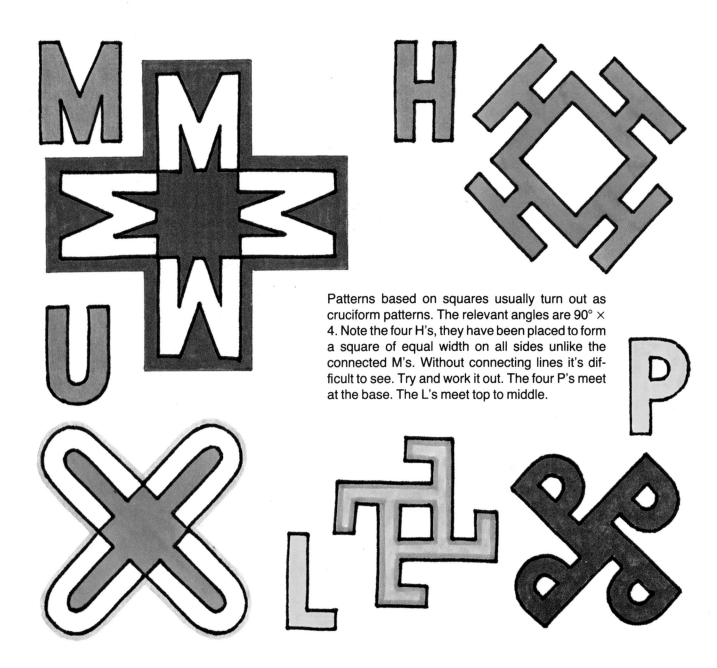

Patterns based on squares usually turn out as cruciform patterns. The relevant angles are 90° × 4. Note the four H's, they have been placed to form a square of equal width on all sides unlike the connected M's. Without connecting lines it's difficult to see. Try and work it out. The four P's meet at the base. The L's meet top to middle.

The pentagon is a five-sided figure. The relevant angles are 72°. The letter K is a versatile letter capable of making interesting patterns. This one seems to have the feel of an actual picture.

The hexagon

On the opposite page the design is based on a six-sided figure – a hexagon. This gives more 'spokes' to the design and causes a gap the same width as the letters. The gaps have been filled with Y's. The letters have been outlined in black on a yellow background and painted with red water-colour. Water-colour is translucent, so the colour will be affected by the background. Had blue water-colour or ink been used instead of red the result would have been green!

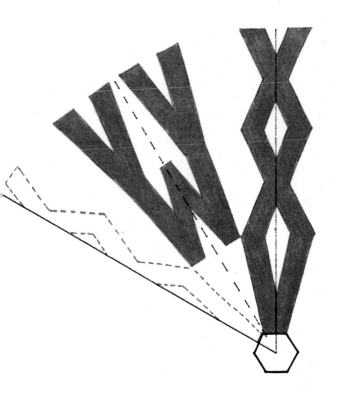

This hexagon pattern is centred with V's. These are topped by an X which is topped by another X extending the pattern to a further perimeter. This leaves large triangular gaps between the six 'spokes'. By filling the gaps with W's topped by two V's the pattern becomes more circular than star-shaped. When designing more complex patterns like this it's useful to work out one of the six sectors of a circled hexagon (sector angle 60°). These can then be reproduced six times to complete the overall pattern.

Overleaf we shall look at positive and negative versions of this pattern and the effects that can be bought about.

It is more difficult to produce a white line drawn by hand than a black one. There are many pens and markers that produce intense black but even today's opaque white markers do not give intense white. White paper collage is one way of getting around this problem. Units of the pattern can be prepared and stuck into position. This wheel pattern has been built up of twelve separate units. These units can be cut out three or four at a time from folded paper. The units are drawn on a medium weight paper and folded so that cuts can be made through the layers. A small craft knife makes the cleanest cutting tool, although scissors will do. After pencilling guide marks (the centre and outer edges on the dark background paper) the units can be stuck down using Latex adhesive, gum or Spray adhesive. When dry, erase the soft pencil marks. Any colouring should be done at this stage using water-colour, ink or soluble markers.

The gradual blending of orange to yellow gives a brighter centre. The black also brightens the colour.

A negative of the design turns the same wheel pattern into something like a stained glass window.

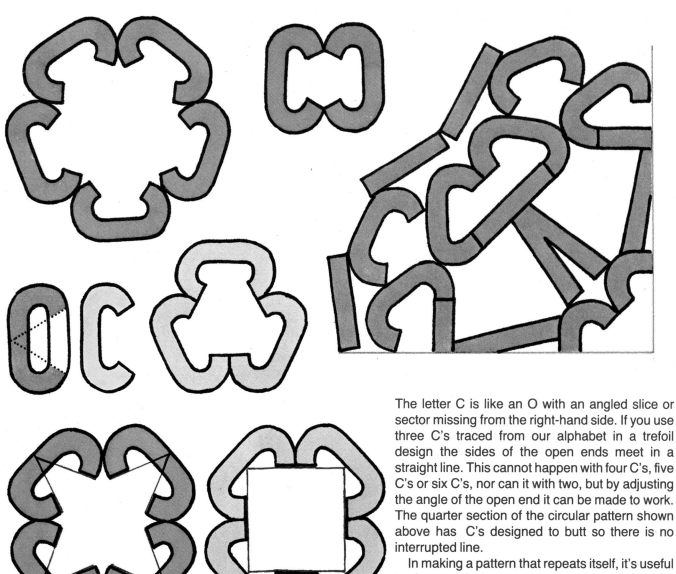

The letter C is like an O with an angled slice or sector missing from the right-hand side. If you use three C's traced from our alphabet in a trefoil design the sides of the open ends meet in a straight line. This cannot happen with four C's, five C's or six C's, nor can it with two, but by adjusting the angle of the open end it can be made to work. The quarter section of the circular pattern shown above has C's designed to butt so there is no interrupted line.

In making a pattern that repeats itself, it's useful to draw up just one section that can be traced repeatedly to complete the design.

In designing a 'wheel' or 'rose' window, to be filled in with transparent colour, I have used a pentagon-shaped centre. Used in conjunction with the five W's it gives a pleasant star shape. By using two I's before the two V's at the circumference, the windows become well balanced and leave small V shapes at the perimeter to finish it off. Perhaps the shapes, reminiscent of space rockets, have made the window look somewhat modern. The design, cut from black card, has been backed with coloured transparent gels to make a practical window. The result can be seen opposite.

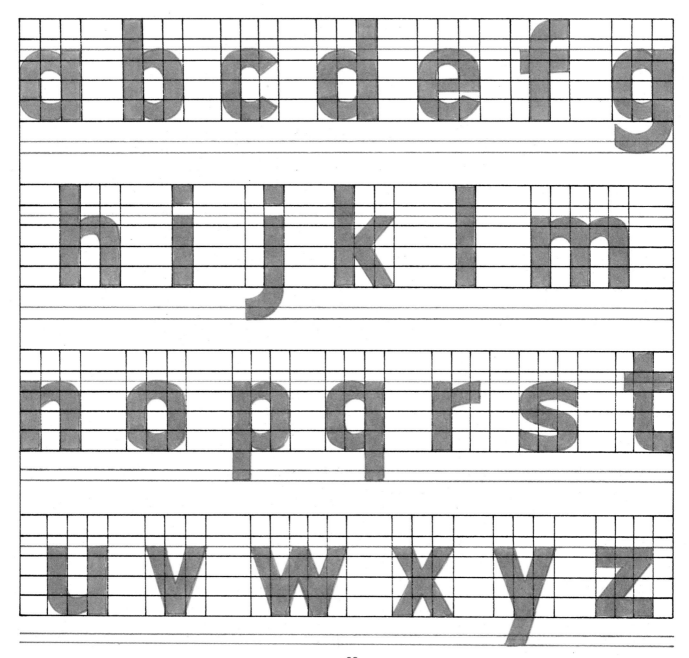

These lower case letters have been designed to be used in conjunction with the capitals. Drawn within the same-shaped squares they can be connected in the same way. The main difference is in the letter height. The basic letter height is three and a half squares. Letters like b, d, f, h etc. have ascenders while g, j, p, q etc. have descenders. These add one and a half squares bringing these letters to the capital height of five squares. The width follows the capitals. The average width is three squares with odd widths for i, j, r, m, and w. The lower case n can be seen as an inverted u. This applies to b and q, also to d and p. The lower case l and the capital I are the same. The lower case letters o, v, w, x, and z are shortened capitals.

a b c d e f g

h i j k l m

n o p q r s t

u v w x y z

The lower case alphabet has, like all our letters, been drawn freehand. These letters have some of the characteristics of the capitals but they also have differences. The letters on the right look the same upside down.

The symmetrical letters shown here are similar to their capitals but whereas the capitals have eleven symmetrical letters the lower case have only six, l being the other. Because the letter width is the same as the capitals they can be connected. For instance, placed sideways, two capital X's could be placed with a lower case x between them.

Lower case letters can be interlocked but not as neatly as capitals. Imagine these examples blacked in. It wouldn't be too difficult to decipher the two m's and h's. The four i's might not be so obvious.

Interesting patterns can be made with just two letters. Coloured or blacked in, they become even more attractive. Placed sideways or diagonally, they start to lose their obvious letter shapes. The last example looks like two capital N's. They are, in fact, two lower case z's.

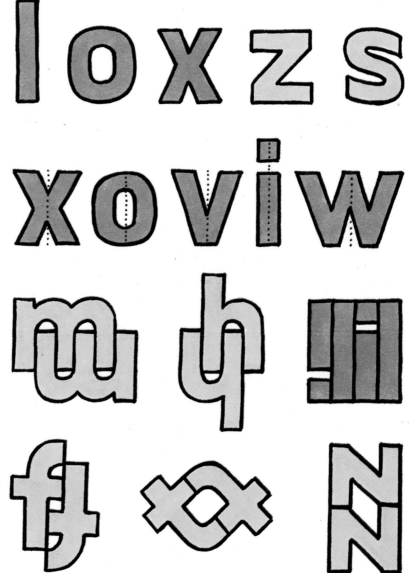

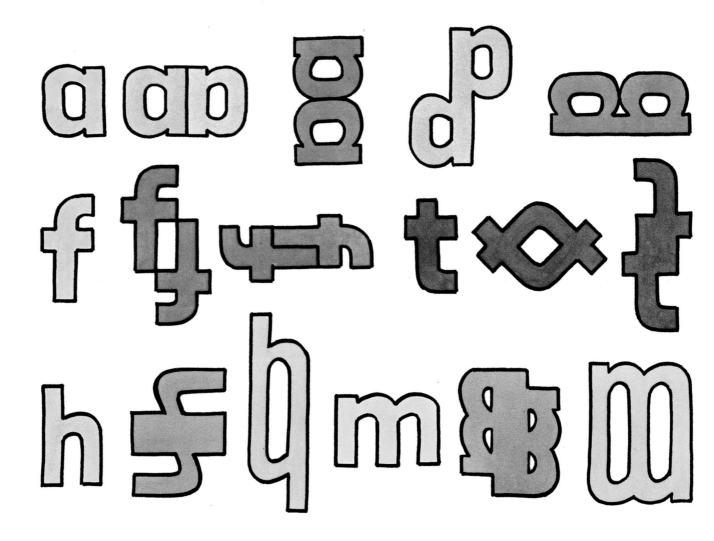

The lower case letters probably provide even more scope for patterns. As with the capital examples, I have drawn up a few shapes on the following pages using two or more letter forms. Later on we shall combine both capitals and lower case letters which gives even more scope for lettercraft. Note the new shapes from letters with ascenders and descenders.

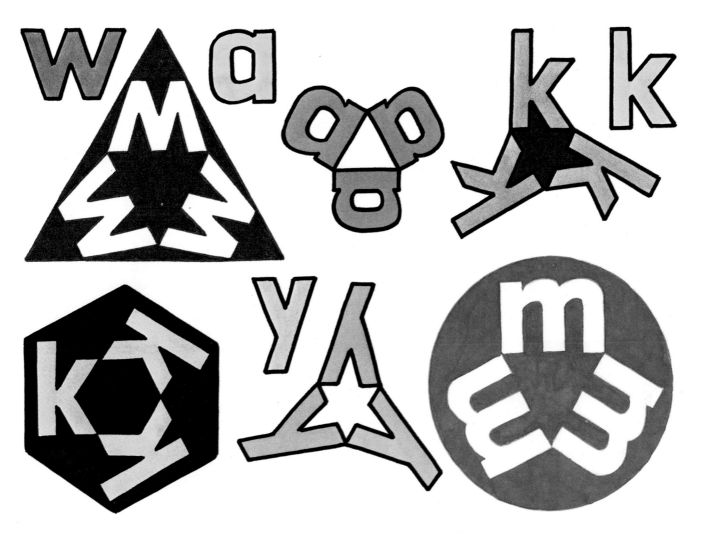

The lower case w is five squares in width. Useful to connect with the m. The capital W, if you check, is four squares in width. Note the rather ugly toothed-shape at the centre of the three pink k's. This doesn't happen with the y's because of the symmetry of the V shape of the y. Positioned another way the three yellow k's have made a hexagon centre.

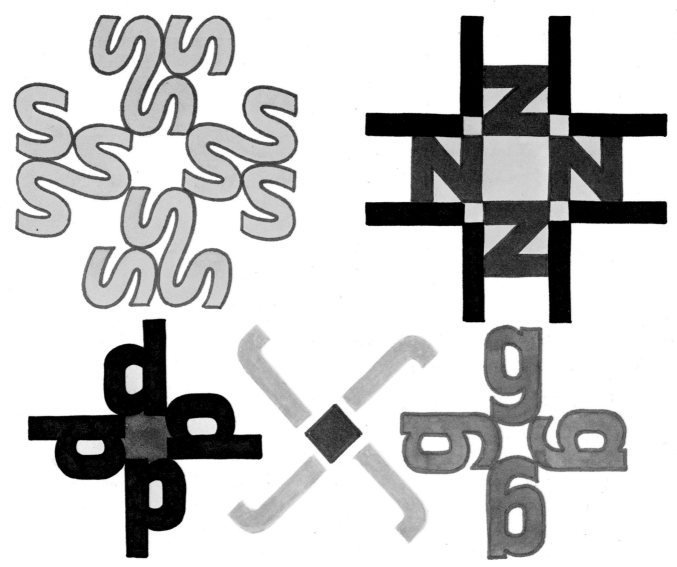

Based on a square the lower case gives great scope for design. Note the centres. See what has happened to the dots of the j's, the shapes made by the g's and d's and the s connection.

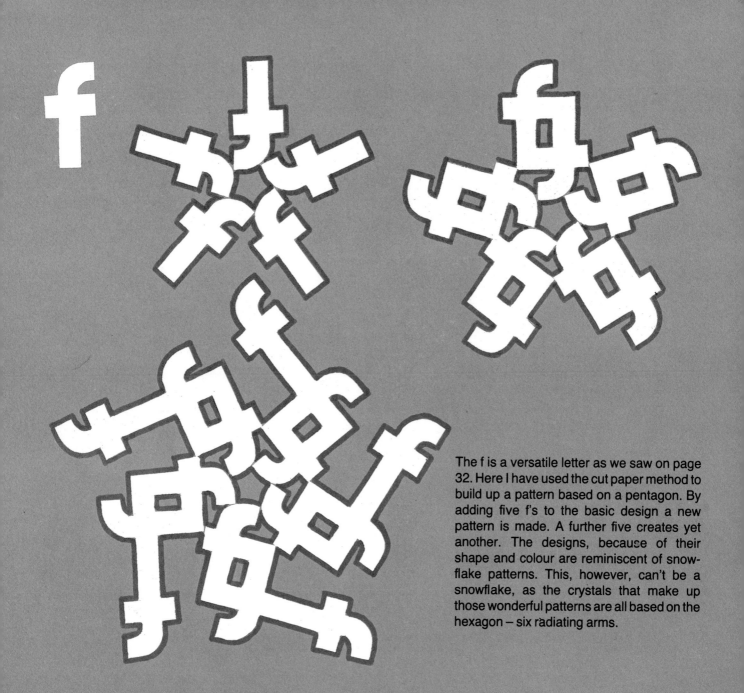

The f is a versatile letter as we saw on page 32. Here I have used the cut paper method to build up a pattern based on a pentagon. By adding five f's to the basic design a new pattern is made. A further five creates yet another. The designs, because of their shape and colour are reminiscent of snowflake patterns. This, however, can't be a snowflake, as the crystals that make up those wonderful patterns are all based on the hexagon – six radiating arms.

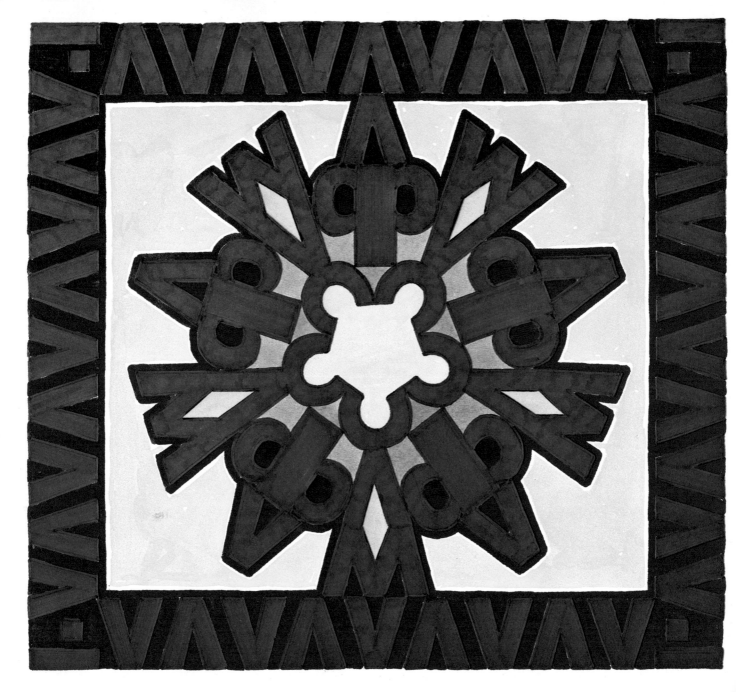

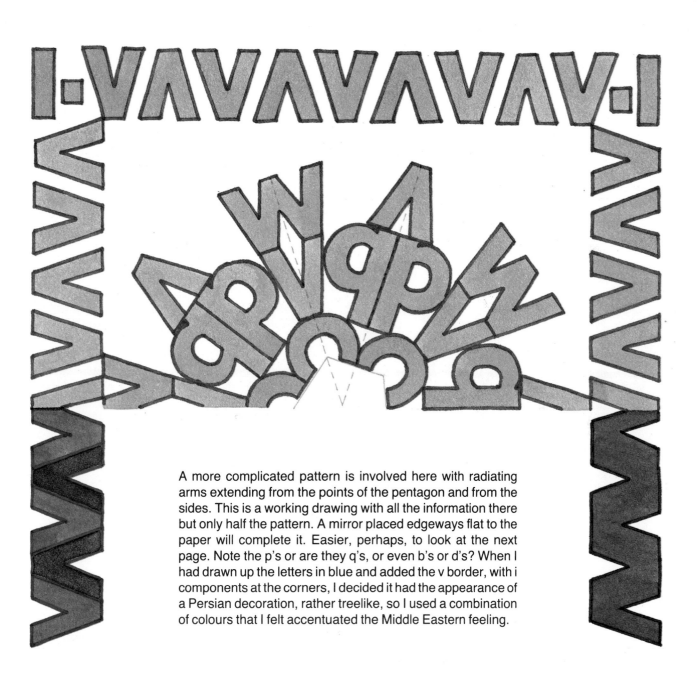

A more complicated pattern is involved here with radiating arms extending from the points of the pentagon and from the sides. This is a working drawing with all the information there but only half the pattern. A mirror placed edgeways flat to the paper will complete it. Easier, perhaps, to look at the next page. Note the p's or are they q's, or even b's or d's? When I had drawn up the letters in blue and added the v border, with i components at the corners, I decided it had the appearance of a Persian decoration, rather treelike, so I used a combination of colours that I felt accentuated the Middle Eastern feeling.

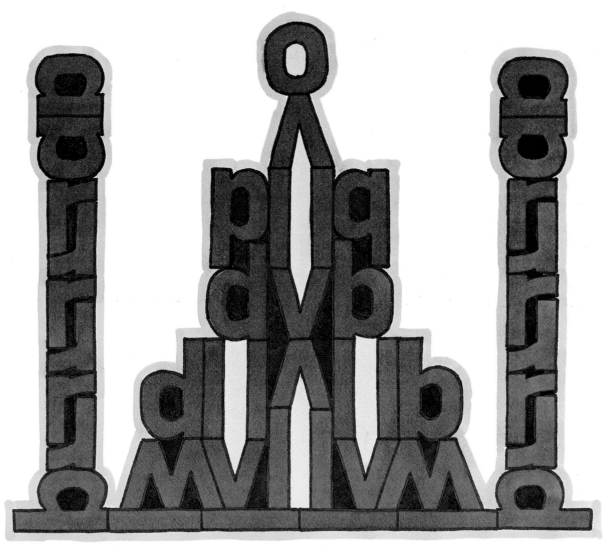

This construction is made up of symmetrical letters: o, v, l, w; pairs that appear symmetric but are different letters: p, q (d, b) and pairs of which one is an inverted r, and pairs of a's, one of which is inverted and both of which are turned sideways.

The overall design is not strictly symmetrical; it would not when divided down the middle reflect itself. Were the r's replaced by l, v, o, x or w it would.

This design, based on a Burmese Temple, is symmetrical save for the s's. To be so, one pair of s's would have to be mirror reflections, unreadable as s's. I have used some licence in the positioning of the four dots from i's in the 'sun' which are incorporated in the design.

On these pages the constructions are strictly symmetrical. Each letter has been positioned in a way that shows its symmetry. On the far left you can see that not only do the letters mirror themselves but the overall design does too. Drawn up without showing the letter connections and with appropriate colour, the design takes on the feeling of a Christmas Card. On the page opposite another symmetric design shows two ways in which it could be treated. Can you work out which lower case letters have been used? The background on the far right has been filled in with scribbled permanent blue marker ink then painted over with a transparent ink.

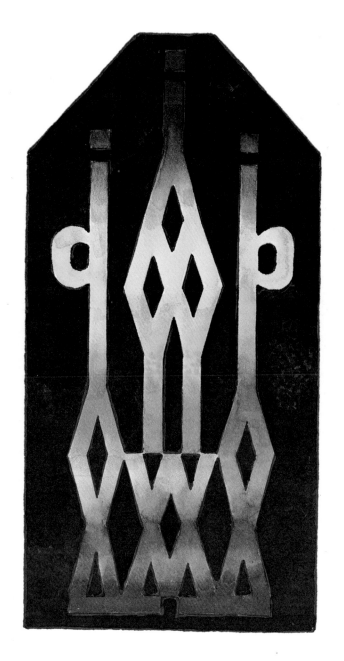

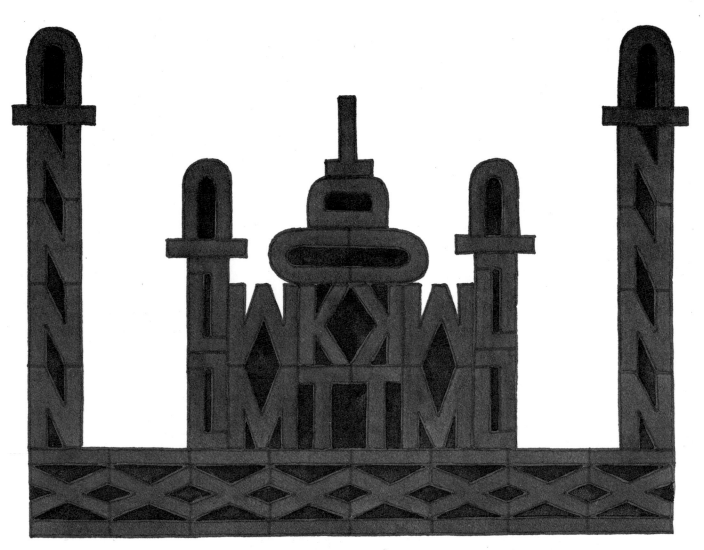

This has the feeling of Mogul India. The construction is made up of capital letters. This has some advantage in that the height and choice of symmetric letters give scope for undreamed of architectural design. It does, however, miss out on the smaller patterns of interest created by using the lower case letters. The colours are typical of 15th century Mogul art.

I have used capital and lower case letters in conjunction for this similar design. The bulk of the construction is the same, but note the use of the lower case a's, x's and i's to create alternative features, which I think improves the design. The odd height, three and a half squares, of the lower case letters has worked out well even when used horizontally in the build up of the design. The fuchsia colours of the first example don't have the contrast of the Indian red and lemon.

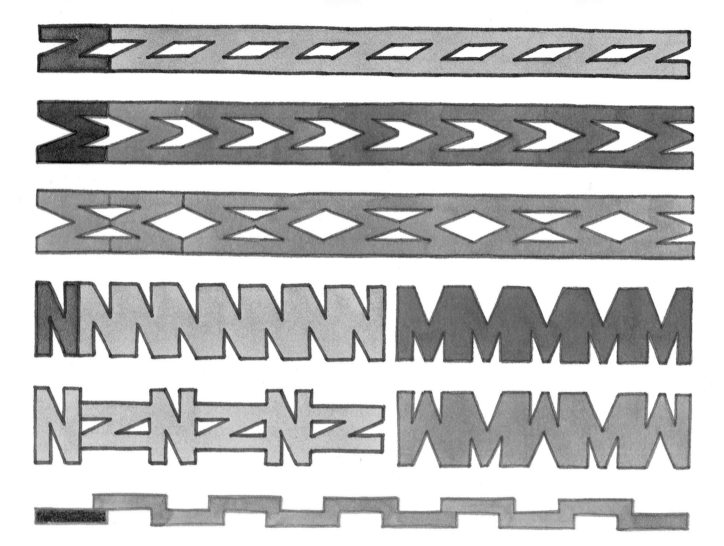

Letters form patterns in varying numbers of units in varying positions. Friezes can be designed by using one or more letter-forms to create a repetitive run. Here I've shown single letters used as a simple repeat. Some are inverted either vertically or horizontally. In all instances the deletion of the connecting lines between letters makes for a more satisfactory pattern. All the letters used in the examples on this page are easy to identify without the left-hand letters.

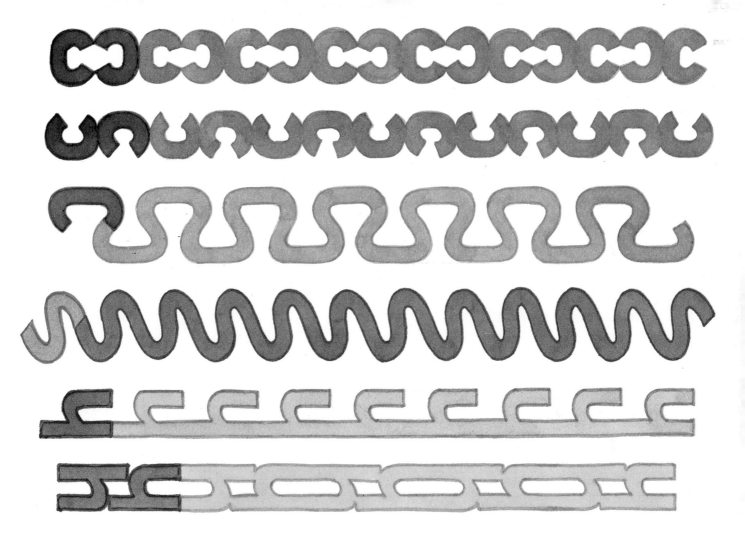

These frieze designs are more complicated. Alternative c's have been inverted making not only mirror images but two ways of looking at the overall pattern. You see pairs of either c's or x's.

The other examples alternate C's with a precise connection. The S example has to be drawn at an angle of 45° to make the run horizontal. The lower case h examples are self explanatory.

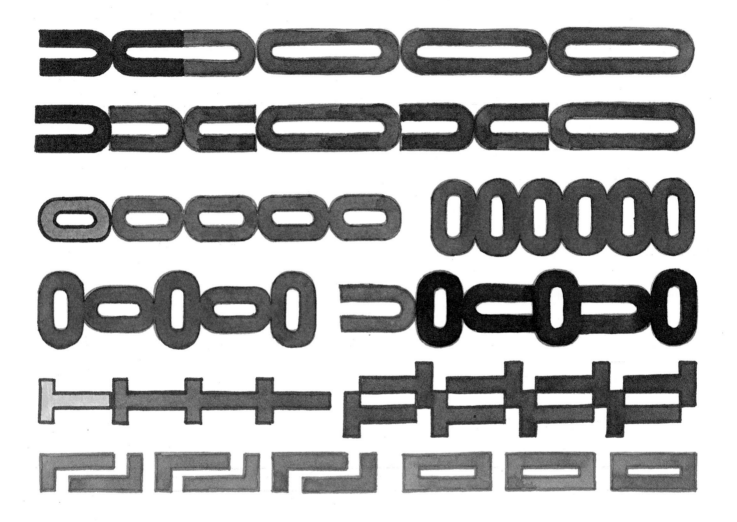

The open end of U can be used to make an extended O. This has a chain link effect. The letter O can be used in a connecting line either placed vertically or horizontally. The larger dark area produced by the former has a bracelet effect while alternating the letters makes an effect like a necklace. The T and L units look angular and hard in comparison with the curved letters.

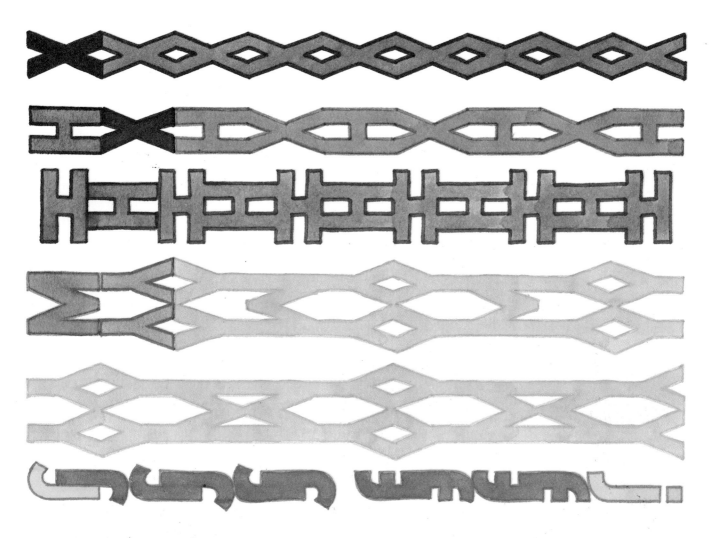

One of the classic frieze units, the X, makes a very useful pattern. Used in conjunction with other broad based units, X always brings about that 'pinched in the middle' effect. H makes good symmetrical patterns used in any combination of positions. Three letter units bring about a wider pattern and could make a rather nice belt. Narrow letters like I, f and j can be used for narrow friezes. In fact there is no f in the bottom line. Look again!

47

Covering repeat patterns

The repeat patterns opposite cover larger areas and are particularly useful for textile designs, fabrics, wallpaper or ornamental openwork such as wrought iron. Before being coloured, the design on the far right (page 49) looked like a tracery for a window or screen from a church or temple. The design is closely patterned with small open spaces between the letter forms. The actual design of T's and H's repeated were virtually impossible to isolate until different colours were used. The largest unit of space in the overall pattern is that coloured yellow. As the pattern made up of the four T's occupies less space than that of the four H's the area of yellow becomes a background and helps to show up the four H and four T square patterns which have their open areas coloured blue, red and orange respectively.

The working drawings on this page show how both designs can be used in different ways. The coloured design here looks more like wallpaper than wrought iron.

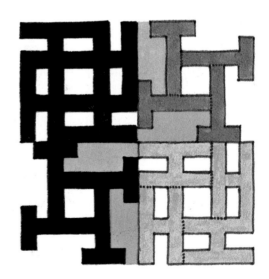

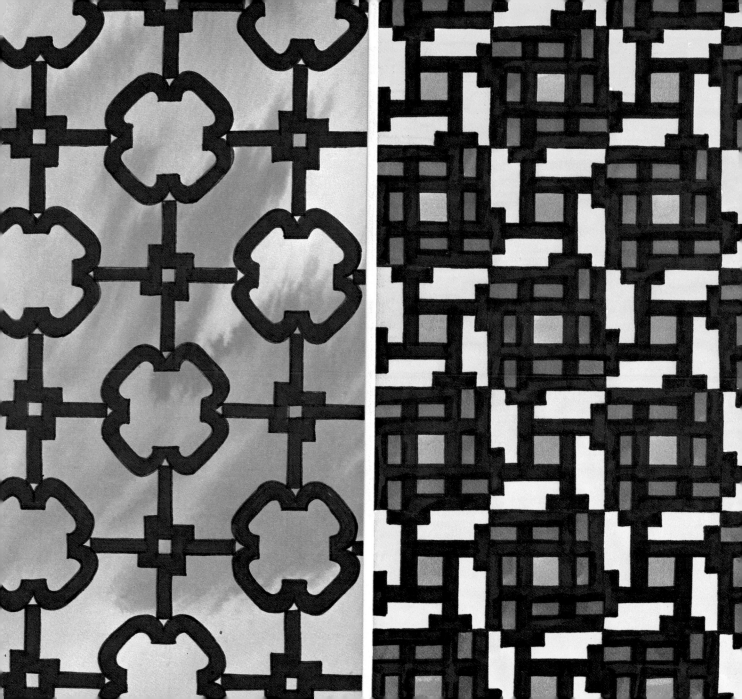

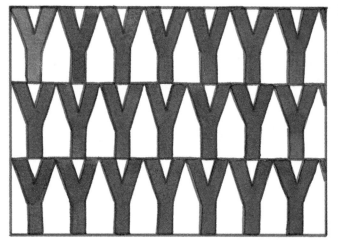

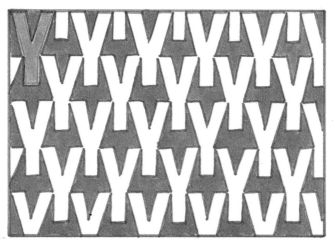

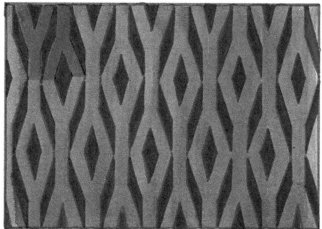

These pages give some idea of the effect of continual repeating of a letter unit or units. An interesting phenomenon is the optical effect of two pattern units being brought about although only one is used. Y, for instance, gives us its own shape alternated by a white shape looking like a church steeple. These examples have been drawn by colouring either the letters or the spaces in between. Your brain can only isolate one unit pattern at a time.

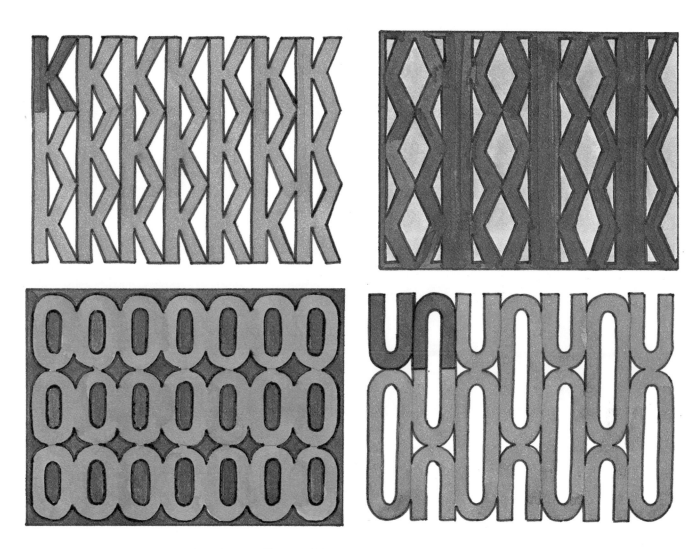

The popular K is seen both upright and inverted. In the upper right-hand example, it is less easy to decipher. If the letter units are drawn in non permanent ink or marker the use of another colour to fill in will cause the colours to run, even if the first colour seems to be dry. This can be seen with the O pattern. U's, connected and half dropped, make another repeat design.

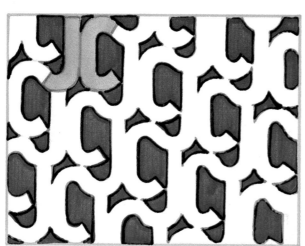

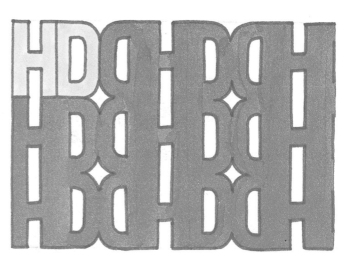

These examples of repeats are all made from two letters. The TH is obvious, especially as the delineating lines are easily seen. WA has a diagonal side connection and makes a less obvious repeat pattern. What happens if we use two W's instead of WA? The inner space is the important factor in the WA and JC repeats. In the last example, inverted D's and correct D's alternate with H.

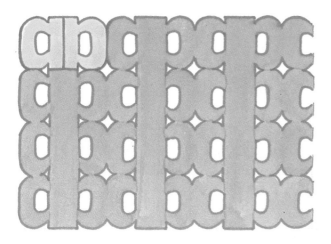

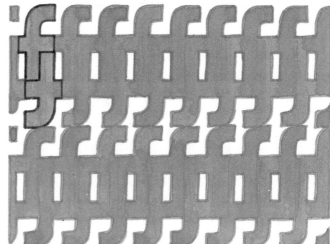

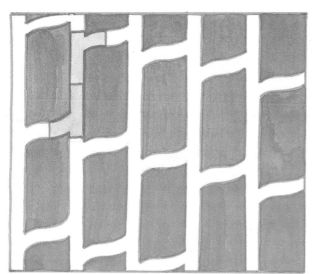

The darker the outline the more obvious the letter units. Compare the top left and bottom right examples with the other two. It would be difficult to establish the letter units in the bottom left example were it not for the two green r's. Note the difference in the overall pattern brought about by the placing of the two f's in the top version compared with those in the version below. The drop of the inverted f in the top version makes quite a difference.

Three ways of designing corners to make decorative frames.   *Opposite:* Combination of picture and frame.

The Lion Tamer . . .
Hat: four L's, two I's
Head: B, two i's, two C's
Body: x, two c's, four V's, three J's, two U's, two a's, six I's

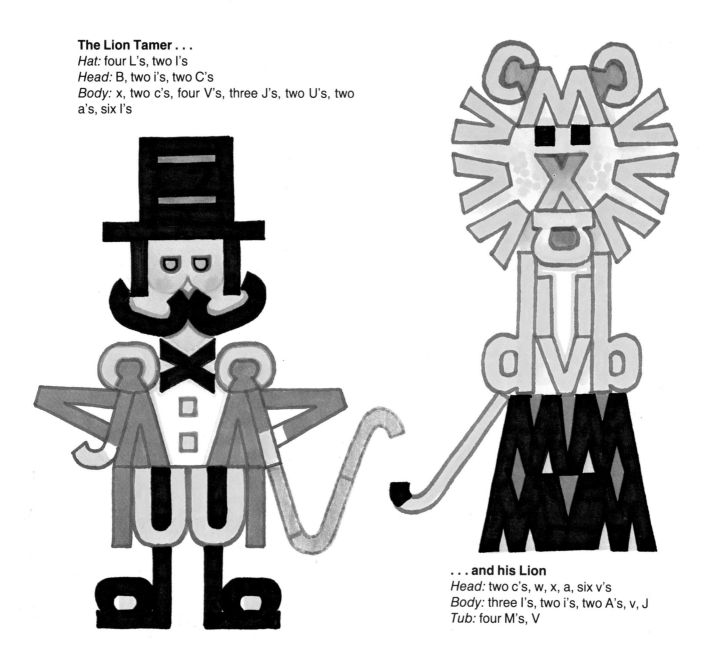

. . . and his Lion
Head: two c's, w, x, a, six v's
Body: three I's, two i's, two A's, v, J
Tub: four M's, V

Illustrating with Lettercraft

So far our designs have been mainly patterns, although the temples, the tree and the windmill show how a stylised form of illustration is not only possible but has a characteristic style of its own. Stylised is the word given to describe a picture that has been drawn with disregard to realism but nevertheless retains sufficient truth for us to recognise the subject. The two examples opposite show us this. I've listed the letters, upper and lower case, used in making the subjects. See if you can work out where they've been placed. The black letters make it quite difficult. This is more difficult than drawing geometric patterns as some degree of imagination is needed. It is surprising how quickly you will find pictures simply by playing about with letters, moving them about until you recognise something. Try it with just O and V. A bird's head? Beak open or shut. It could be a gnome's hat. Add M, two T's and two V's and you have the whole gnome!

The following four pages have illustrations made with letters all of the same size. Later we shall be varying the sizes of the letters within the same picture. This makes for easier creativity.

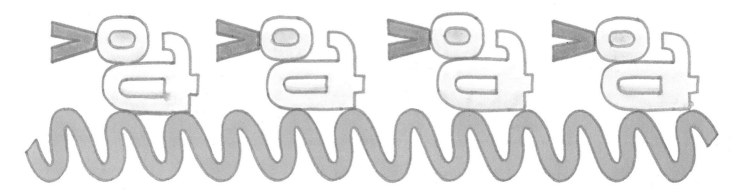

Clown
Hat: V, A, two i's
Head: two v's, T, two a's, c (dots from i)

Ruff: eleven J's
Body: two of each: c, V, w, D, E, four M's, and an I.

Aircraft
A, three H's, four E's, two of each: i, v and V.
Speed lines: thirteen I's

Clouds: ten C's
Buildings: ten I's, five i's, two T's, three v's, seven H's.

Engine: two of each: T, H, I, I, P, B, E
Tender: two M's, two P's
Coaches: ten L's, six E's, three I's, two B's
Smoke: three O's, three C's
Church: three I's, an E and a V.

Here is a list of the letters used to make up this train. They are quite easy to identify. L has been very useful!

The background texture has been made by scribble put on with water-colour paint sticks.

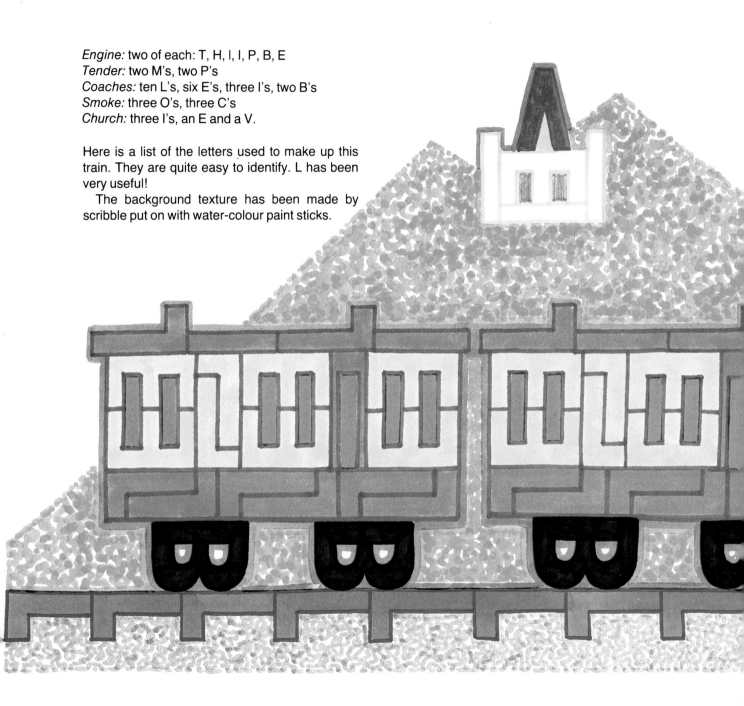

This picture, and that on the opposite page, differ from previous illustrations in that some letter forms are overlapping. All are recognisable but some are not fully seen. In the 'flower' picture outlining has been done in both black and in colours. In this case, I think that either black or coloured outlines should be used but not mixed. This page contains another feature. Letter sizes vary from large H to tiny v's. This gives even more scope for creative drawing.

The illustration on this page is made up from letters of varying size, some of which overlap. This is effective in producing results like the woodman's goggles (B) and the hand holding the axe (JJ). The slant of the letters (PU) in the hat and head make a less mechanical feeling to the drawing.

On the opposite page, the letters making up Father Christmas have been cut from paper and stuck down, making a collage. This gives a clean cut appearance without having to outline the letters. The body is a large A overlapped with: three I's, O, U, two c's, m. The remaining letters are: V, I, o, two T's and 2 D's.

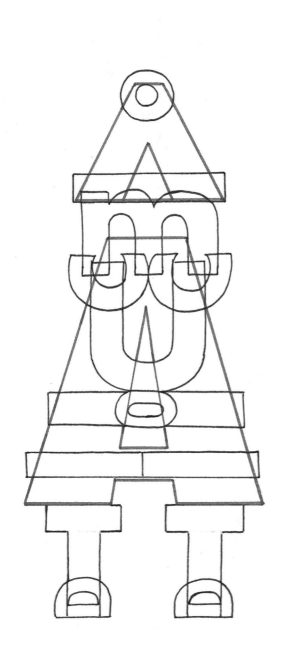

Distorting letters

Here is a way of using our imagination to create characters by distorting the more usual letter forms. We have often seen letters like my rounded k in advertising. It is still easily seen as k, but our imagination can see it as something else with the addition of a few extra lines! The R and C only needs a slight rearrangement to become a rabbit. The softening and distortion of the original letters and the addition of eye and whiskers completes the metamorphosis.

The three creatures shown here are made up with distorted letters that are still readable as letters. The letters used actually spell out the name of the character they represent. The O of the sun works well with its orange centre but the O of the Hippo's body has been filled in with body colour otherwise it might be taken for a Henry Moore sculpture!

Cat: three V's, three D's, I, A, C.   *King:* Two X's, W, four I's, five a's, U, L, 3 O's, three C's, V, two D's, two J's, H.   *Throne:* three I's, V, O.

Here is a *House Mouse*.
He's made from two O's,
two C's for his ears
and a V for his nose.
d and b for the rest
Except for that S.
It gives him a tail
Which is what you'd suppose.

Zoologists on the telly can
Tell you about the pelican.

Pelican: P, two D's, V, two L's, O.
Fish: X, W.
TV: two L's.
Zoologist: U, two I's, two C's, two V's, O.

R's, B's and P's
make rabbits (with V's)

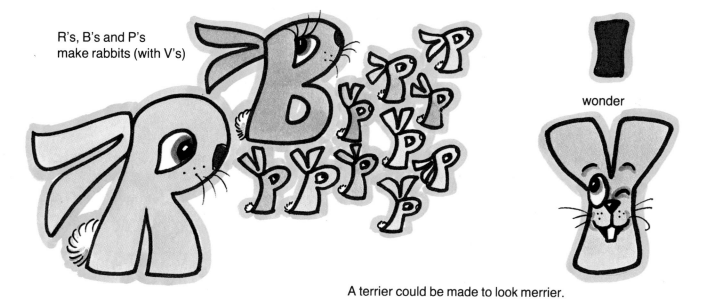

I
wonder

A terrier could be made to look merrier.

Puppies can be drawn with E's
. . . . . so can B ee S!

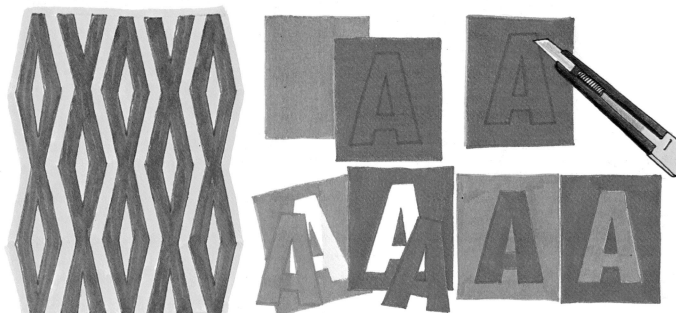

Simulated marquetry

Marquetry is the craft of inlaying different pieces of wood to make a pattern composed entirely of wood. Contrasts are effected by the colour and grain of the pieces. Simple, clean cut letters are particularly effective. We could use real wood or we could simulate the colours and grain pattern of wood by drawing and painting them on paper and using that instead. The sensible way to make the cut pieces fit properly is to take two contrasting pieces of paper, lay one on top of the other and cut, with a craft knife, both pieces at once. This gives you two identical letters and two backgrounds. These can be alternated to make the best contrast. The drawings here in red and orange show you what to do. If you draw wood grain on paper you can use this with one piece at right angles to the other. You can see how the wood grain makes its own contrast. The photograph shows simulated wood grain, made of adhesive plastic, used to cover a wooden box. This plastic can be bought in rolls from DIY shops.

Paper Cups and Plates

I've chosen the two C's as a unit of design from which these three patterns can be made to paint on paper plates and cups. Permanent markers are very good for these as paper plates are sometimes made from card with a grease-proof covering which will only take coloured marker ink. The plates could actually be used as plates, but I don't think they'd last too long! It is better to use them for decorations.

To find out how many times your unit of design will fit round a circle you need to find the circumference of the inner circle by using the formula $2\pi r$, where π (pi) = 3.142, r = radius (a line from the centre to the edge of the circle). In this case the radius = 36mm so the formula is $2 \times 3.142 \times 36$. This = 226.2mm. Now divide the circumference, 226.2 by the width of the design unit which is 20mm. So the answer is 11.3 times. 0.3mm is so tiny you can ignore it for the design.

It's no more difficult to paint lettercraft on china than on paper plates. The difficulty is in marking the china with your design before painting. A chinagraph pencil is fine, but we usually need to trace our designs from the working drawing done in pencil. I have found a way of doing this. Rub coloured chalk dust over the back of the pencil drawing then rub coloured wax crayon over that. Stick the paper to the china with tiny dabs of Latex adhesive. If the plate is not flat you cut between pairs of letters so that the flaps made will conform to the curve of the surface. Now you can trace the pattern with a hard pencil. The guide marks will be seen easily. After painting, the surplus marks can be rubbed off with white spirit after the paint is quite dry. I have used a solvent-based paint from Pēbēo, who make craft paints for every surface you can think of; they also make a water-based ceramic paint, which needs to be baked when dry.

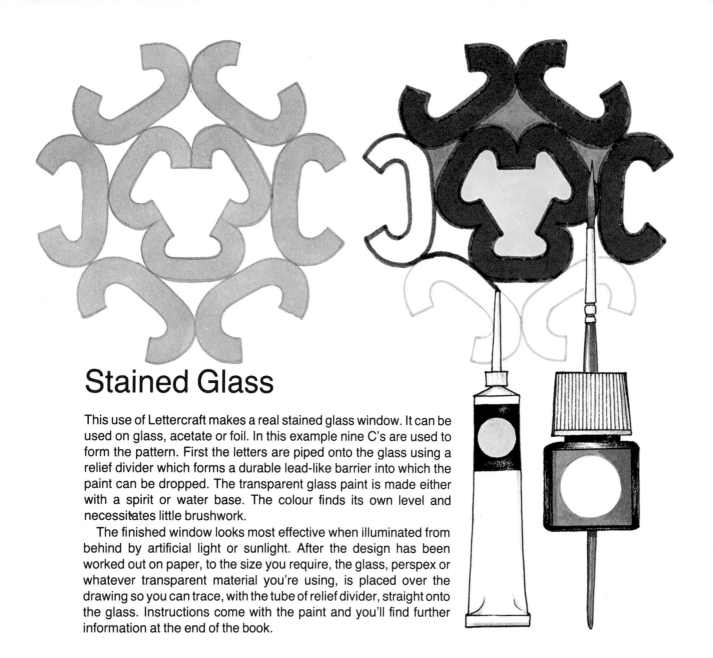

Stained Glass

This use of Lettercraft makes a real stained glass window. It can be used on glass, acetate or foil. In this example nine C's are used to form the pattern. First the letters are piped onto the glass using a relief divider which forms a durable lead-like barrier into which the paint can be dropped. The transparent glass paint is made either with a spirit or water base. The colour finds its own level and necessitates little brushwork.

The finished window looks most effective when illuminated from behind by artificial light or sunlight. After the design has been worked out on paper, to the size you require, the glass, perspex or whatever transparent material you're using, is placed over the drawing so you can trace, with the tube of relief divider, straight onto the glass. Instructions come with the paint and you'll find further information at the end of the book.

Foil Relief

This picture has been drawn on paper, placed over foil, and traced firmly with a ballpoint pen. Providing folded newspaper is placed beneath foil, the tracing will indent the foil and when finished the original picture will be seen on the foil as a series of indented lines. Turn the foil over and you have a relief picture and a mirror image. This you can see in the photograph. Here I have cut out the foil along the skyline and replaced it with oven foil that had been crumpled then smoothed out to give a textured effect. Pictures on foil can be painted with transparent glass paint.

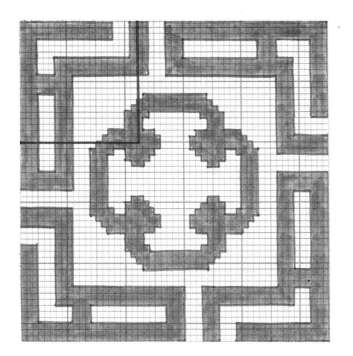

Embroidery

Embroidery is made up of stitches on a canvas backing. Because the canvas is made up of tiny squares the pattern has to be made up of squares. A curve would have to be a shape of steps. The L follows the squares because the L is right angled. The C has to follow the squares and so looks rather odd, but this is the charm of this sort of embroidery. We can't just fill in a square like a mosaic, the stitches have to be put in diagonally over the cross where four squares meet. The enlarged diagram shows this method of stitching. You need to start one square outside the marked pattern. It needs four needle holes in four squares to put three stitches in three squares. The wool is thicker than shown in my diagram and would completely cover the marked area of the canvas.

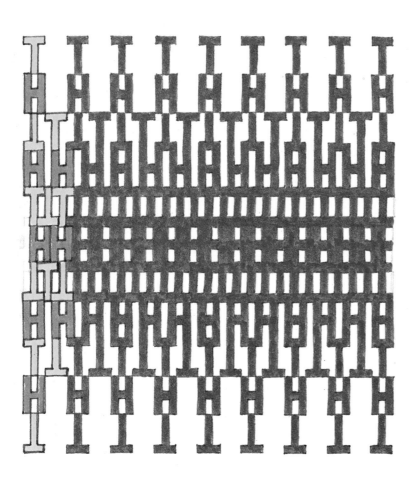

Knitwear

The cover of this book shows me wearing a pullover with decorative bands made up from the letters TH. It looks more complicated than it is. Drawn up you see that each line has alternate T's and H's positioned in different ways. The centre of the pattern has the darkest area and is made up of connecting H's.

It is easier to draw such a design on graph paper with T occupying seven tiny squares and H eleven. Converted to knitting, each square would be shown as a V shape of wool, so the letters have the characteristic shape of all knitting patterns. You see this in the photograph opposite.

Ann Ratcliffe, a lecturer in crochet and knitwear, made two pullovers from my designs. One for the cover and this one with a narrow band, shown here above, and right, the main design.

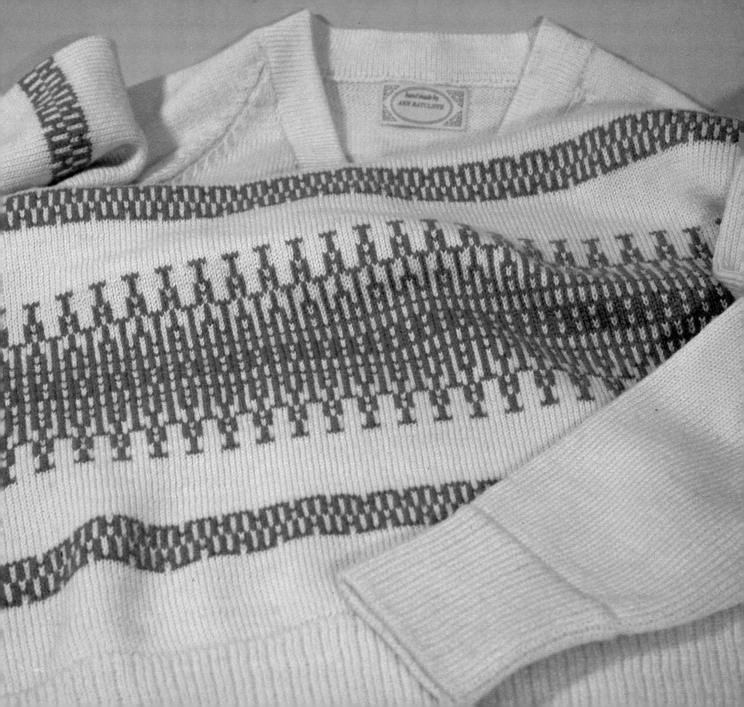

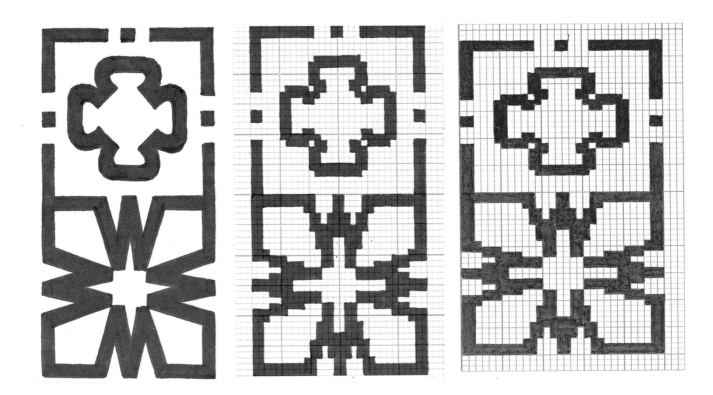

Machine Knitting

A conversion of the original design for knitwear is necessary, as not only will the design be made up of small units but it will also, if machine knitted, have to be converted again from tiny square units to small rectangular units. If a square is represented by 10 × 10 these rectangles would measure approximately 9 × 11. This makes a distortion for which it is sometimes possible to compensate. However, this distortion is particularly useful in knitwear as it allows for the garment stretching over the body when worn. It will be seen, as with embroidery, that the squared pattern is a far cry from the original Lettercraft design. This is the delightful characteristic of all knitted, woven and embroidered material because these are media of stitches, not brush or pen.

Once again Ann Ratcliffe has used my design to produce this knitted jacket with the CW motif for Carolyn Williams, who is seen here modelling it.

Simulated Embroidery

Instead of using silk, cotton or wool to embroider a picture, it is possible to use a special paint on fabric that can, under certain conditions, look rather like embroidery. You can use the paint straight from the tube or you can use it with a brush. It can also be diluted with water. Used straight from the tube, it becomes rather like icing a cake, using the nozzle on the tube in exactly the same way. When the paint is dry, you turn your work face down onto a padding of folded towels or some other thick, soft fabric and iron it. When ironed briefly at the right temperature, the paint expands giving a remarkably effective result. All

instructions come with the paint. You'll find useful names and addresses at the end of the book. In the photograph opposite I've used various colours piped onto white cotton fabric. The light green of the cat's eyes and his bow have been brushed in, so have his pink nose and his orange markings, using paint which was diluted with water. After the ironing process, I cut round the outline of my cat and stuck him onto a dishcloth, a rectangle of which I'd painted green with fabric paint. A border of piping in three colours framed and completed the picture.

Painting On Fabric

Fabric paint can be used with either brush or marker. Pēbēo make coloured refillable felt tip markers that are used like any other marker. The paint is made laundry fast by ironing the finished design when dry. Tight woven and starched materials are easy to draw on. Softer, woolly materials require a dabbing action with the marker to get the best result. I drew this design on a T-shirt for my granddaughter, Hattie. The letters of her name are incorporated in the design. In this case the letters are obvious, but there is an alternative as you will see in the top left design.

Ceramics

We've seen that pottery can be decorated with Lettercraft. Pottery can also be made of Lettercraft. The way to make pottery letters, or a design of letters, is to roll out clay and cut out the letters just as if making pastry. The letters must first be drawn on cardboard and cut out so you can press them lightly onto the rolled out clay. This will give you enough indication of where to cut. A small long-bladed craft knife is ideal for this. Letters can be as thick or as thin as you wish and mounted on another piece of clay before drying hard. A ceramic paint can then be used to give a glazed effect to the finished work.

Clay Impress

Clay or plastic modelling compound can be indented with wood or cardboard letters to make an impression. The clay is rolled out like pastry. A bottle makes an excellent rolling pin. The cut-out letter forms are then pressed into the clay to a depth of 1 or 2 mm. The point of a penknife or small craft knife will help to lift the card letter from the clay without further marking it. Fingers, however carefully used, are liable to make more impressions! A neater and more interesting design will result if you leave small channels between the letters making up the design or pattern. Work out a drawing first so that you know what letters are needed. You will need only one of each letter as they can be used many times. Those of mine have been cut with a craft knife from 2 mm thick card. I needed one each of V, v, a, I, M, U, L and D. Using the cutout letters, copy the drawing straight onto the clay. You could lay the straight edge of paper on the clay to get the first straight line of letters but be careful not to press it into the clay. There really is no need to mark the clay in any way other than with your chosen letters. Depending on the thickness of the clay block it will take about forty-eight hours to set hard. If you wish it can then be polished with shoe polish.

Costume Jewellery

Many of our smaller patterns and designs, made up of letters, are suitable for converting into costume jewellery. Medallions, brooches, and pendants can be made quite easily using one or other of the plastic modelling compounds that may be bought from craft shops. If you are keen on Metalwork you'll find Lettercraft suitable for that too. Personalised jewellery, made with the initials of the person receiving it worked into the design, is always welcome. For school plays, especially historical plays, you can all become jewellery designers! Synthetic modelling material like 'Fimo'

can be made pliable and shaped or cut into the forms required. It can even be hardened into a durable plastic by baking the finished work in a kitchen oven for about 20 minutes at a temperature of 120°C. It can then be varnished or painted. I made up the four designs seen here. It was not very difficult. Like other modelling materials, this can be rolled out flat so that shapes can be cut from it. You can use a small craft knife for this or a simple wooden tool which younger people may find easier to cope with. The oven process would, of course, need to be done under supervision.

Prints and Print Making

Any solid, flat surface will transfer ink or paint to paper, so you have a wide choice of material from which to make a block to print. These letters have been printed from a cardboard cut-out covered with adhesive plastic tape. They have been stuck onto a wood block, which makes printing easier. Poster paint can be brushed or dabbed onto the block which is then pressed by hand to the paper. Lino is a more durable material for block making. Lino and cutting tools can be bought from art and craft shops, where you will also find water or oil-based tubes of printing ink and rollers.

Remember that anything printed will give a mirror image so letters like N, B, and D, must be stuck to the wood block the wrong way round. The N shows you what I mean. Paint doesn't give such a dense print as printing ink does, nevertheless I very much like the textured result from card and paint on this page. Compare these with the lino cut on the following pages.

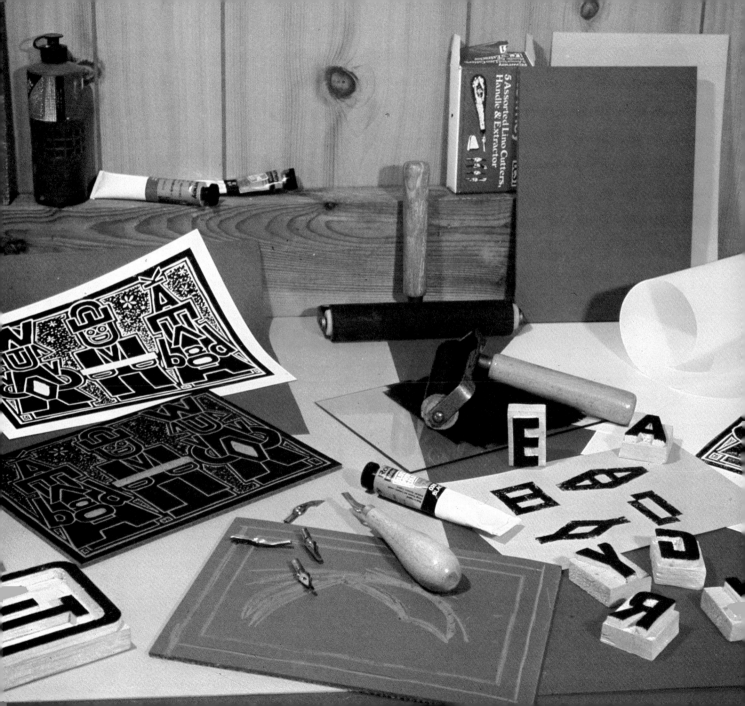

Letters of varying size have been used to make the 'Three Kings', a colourful illustration that would lend itself as a design for a Christmas card. There is no black in the design. The colours have been chosen to make the figures stand out. The blue textured background helps to do this, as well as the light orange colour bordering the figures.

Lino cuts make excellent greetings and Christmas cards. The 'Three Kings' have been altered only slightly to make the block for this print. I think the economic use of the red is quite effective. After printing as many cards as you want, you could hand-colour them as I've done.

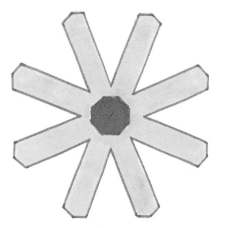

The much thinner letters from which these designs were made, from the alphabet on the other page, give far larger inner spaces to the closed letter forms. This enables the forms to be filled with colour and gives a different effect from the designs shown earlier. It makes an interesting change.

ABCDEFG
HIJKLM
NOPQRST
UVWXYZ

Alternative Alphabet

Here is a useful alternative alphabet for Lettercraft. These letters are almost half the width of those we've been using for pattern making. Every letter, except I, occupies the height and width of a square. Letter I is one × eight so a grid of squares in which to draw the letters is made up of sixty four tiny squares. The advantages for certain designs can be seen on the opposite page.

Dry Transfers

These sheets of letters, both capital and lower case, can be bought from art shops, some stationers and graphic suppliers. There is an enormous choice of type faces. They are expensive, but if you know anyone who uses them professionally you may be lucky enough to pick up some of the sheets that still have some letters that have not been used. Q, X and Z seems to get left on most of mine but I doubt if you'll find any E's since it's the most used letter in the English language. You place the transparent sheet over the paper where you want the chosen letter transferred and rub the letter with a soft pencil or ballpoint until it appears on the paper. Graphic artists use them instead of hand drawing letters. I've found that neat patterns can be made using them.

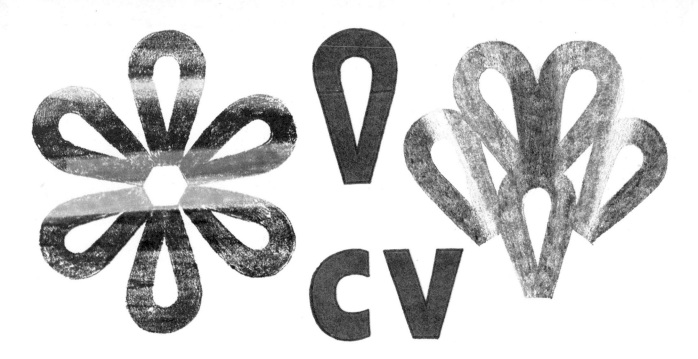

'Do it Yourself' Dry Transfer

We have seen that coloured chalk rubbed on the back of a drawing can be used to transfer the drawing to another piece of paper, card or other flat surfaces by tracing with a hard pencil. In the same way, a piece of thin paper can be rubbed with multi-coloured chalks to form a sort of colourful 'carbon paper' and used in the same way. Letter patterns and designs may then be used in conjunction with your coloured 'carbon paper' to make multi-coloured designs by outlining and filling in while tracing. Use a hard pencil to outline, then a less hard one to fill in. An HB is good for this, and by filling in the letter outlines you can see where you've got to. It's a good idea to anchor the papers in use with paper masking tape so that nothing slips to spoil all your hard work. Chalk gives a less bright effect than wax crayon or oil pastel. The latter is used in the same way, but the paper on which you put the coloured crayon must be waxed paper, greaseproof paper, or the sort that you find in cereal packets, which is very good for the purpose. Wax crayon and oil pastel will not rub off from ordinary paper. The design top left is from oil pastel and the other is from chalk. The photograph shows the materials that have been used along with another, larger, pattern.

Materials and Where to Find Them

The purpose of this book is twofold: to entertain you with the actual doing and end results of my, and subsequently I hope your, efforts and to provide you with a new and satisfying way of pattern making that can be applied to many crafts.

Mostly you will only need the simplest of drawing and colouring materials, which you will probably already have at home: marker pens, water colours and paper – and some of you will get by quite happily with nothing other than these. However, I do receive a number of letters from people who have watched me at work on television, and although I have mentioned the materials I was using, they have been unable to find them in their local shops. Some of the projects in the book require special paints or other media to achieve the best effect and I have therefore listed those you could have difficulty in tracing. The manufacturers will give you the name of your nearest stockists.

Small stationers usually have a good selection of markers and probably also stock pencils, ink and paper, but for a wider selection you must find an art shop or one of the bigger stationers like W. H. Smith and Son Ltd.

In your home town you should have few problems in finding what you need. British Telecom's Yellow Pages are helpful in listing stockists under Graphic Art Materials, Craft Materials, Drawing Office Equipment, Hobby Shops and Do It Yourself Shops. Wool shops provide wool for knitting and embroidery and may also stock tapestry canvas; if not, try a departmental store. For printing inks, rollers and other more specialized materials you will need to visit an Art and Craft Shop.

Materials available from W. H. Smith and Son Ltd

Hard and soft pencils
General purpose inks
Pens and marker pens (permanent and non permanent)
Brushes
Water-colours
Wax crayons and oil pastels
Chalks
Paper of various weights
Colour cards and papers
Graph paper
Erasers
Rulers
Protractors
T-squares

Other materials

Painting on China (page 76) Ceramic Paint, Pêbêo. A. West and Partners Limited, 684 Mitcham Road, Croydon CR9 3AB.
Stained Glass (page 78) Relief Outline and Stained Glass Paint from Pêbêo

Metal Foil Relief (page 80) Oven Foil from Super markets. Art Foil from Pēbēo

Simulated Embroidery (page 88) Expanding paint. 'Brod Express' from Pēbēo

Painting on Fabric (page 90) Setaskrib Markers from Pēbēo

Costume Jewellery (page 96) Modelling Compound is 'FIMO' (Eberhard Faber) from Art and Craft Shops

Simulated Wood Grain (page 72) Fablon Surface Adhesive from Do It Yourself Shops

The Markers, Permanent and Non Permanent, of different sizes, used in the book came from Conté. Conté (UK) Limited, Park Farm Industrial Estate, Park Farm Road, Folkestone, Kent CT19 5EY.